HILLSDALE BOOK

LOCATION OF 23RD AND SCOTT ⊕

WHERE NICK
PARKED HIS
RED VALIANT
⊕

KIDS WE HATED
LIVED SOMEWHERE
IN HERE
⊕

THE TIMS HOUSE,
FIRST HOUSE
IN HILLSDALE
⊕

WHERE LORNE
PLANTED THE
EARTHWORMS

ORIGINAL
DRIVEWAY
ON LAMONT

ONE OF A
HUNDRED
STUMPS
⊕

WHERE THE SEDIMENTS
GATHER TO PRACTICE
⊕

UNCLE TO
MONTE
⊕

⊕ MANHOLE ON MCNAB

⊕ "THE ROAD THAT ISN'T"

PIANO TEACHER'S HOUSE ⊕

The Man From Saskatchewan, Book Five

HILLSDALE BOOK

GERALD HILL

NeWest Press

Library and Archives Canada Cataloguing in Publication

Hill, Gerald, 1951–, author
Hillsdale book / Gerald Hill.

Includes bibliographical references. ISBN 978-1-927063-81-1 (pbk.)

1. Regina (Sask.) — Poetry. I. Title.

PS8565.I443H55 2015   C811'.54   C2014-906470-5

Editor: Don Kerr
Author photo: Mark Anderson

NeWest Press acknowledges the support of the Canada Council for the Arts, the Alberta Foundation for the Arts, and the Edmonton Arts Council for support of our publishing program. We acknowledge the financial support of the Government of Canada through the Canada Book Fund for our publishing activities.

#201, 8540 – 109 Street
Edmonton, Alberta t6g 1e6
780.432.9427
www.newestpress.com

NeWest Press

No bison were harmed in the making of this book.

Printed and bound in Canada

It is also necessary to have no philosophy.
With philosophy there are no trees, just ideas.
— **FERNANDO PESSOA (ALBERTO CAEIRO)**, *Detached Poems*

Maybe I should comb my hair
the way I did in high school?
— **GEORGE BOWERING**, *Kerrisdale Elegies*

But to whom does the solitary traveller make reply?
— **VIRGINIA WOOLF**, *Mrs. Dalloway*

Contents

Foreword

You are entering Hillsdale, a southern suburb of Regina. Opened to its first few houses in 1956, Hillsdale was a modern suburb, in the mid-'50s sense of modern urban design. As if protecting two sensibilities, the car and the family, the design featured perimeter through-streets and a snarl of interior bays, crescents, and cul-de-sacs.

I moved to Hillsdale with my parents and sisters in 1961. I moved there again, with my own family this time, in 1995.

By 2008 Hillsdale becomes a textual field on which a boy (1961—1972), and a man (1995—2010) and a traveller (as ever) arrive and leave, return and leave, figuring who and where they are. It becomes a document faithfully received, playfully rendered.

Laid out as streets and crescents on annexed farmland, Hillsdale becomes text and images laid out in this book.

Hillsdale welcomes you.

GERALD HILL
Regina, Saskatchewan

Figures

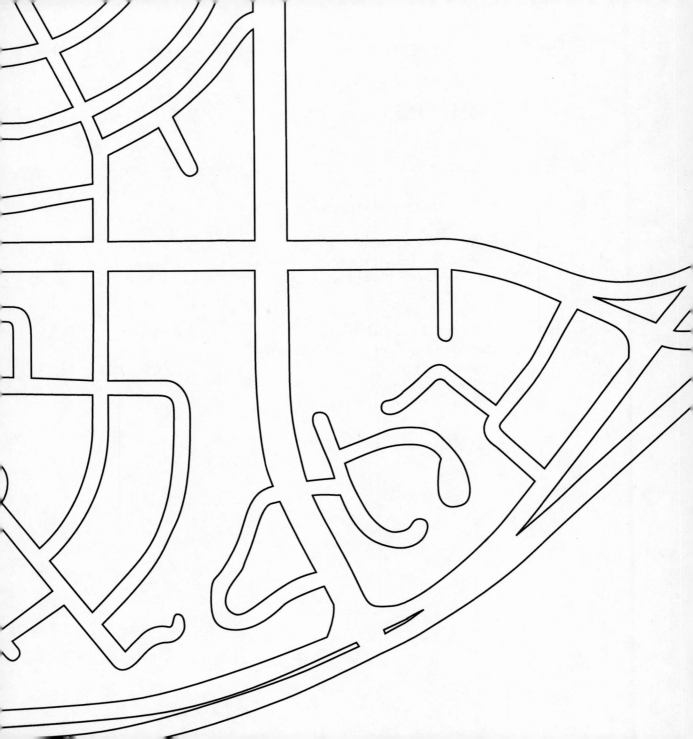

GROWVERTURE: PORTRAIT OF THE SUBURB AS A YOUNG TOWN

for the Town of Hillsdale
Regina
Saskatchewan
North-West Territories
Treaty 4 Land
Rupert's Land
Precambrian basement
Back Up

+

hear the sisters inside
with their cute friend
Gloria

after school
the Stooges came on
and the moms came home

and the dads came home
and called you home
and you had to

+

happy hour dads
get home right
now Ron walks

to Ralph's place Ralph
pours him a rum
and Coke Ron

calls Doris who says
just a minute puts
beans and wieners on

for the kids *do your*
homework no tv we're at
the Gilliams' rums pour

adults argue
drunk outside some
poor kid's room

+

we have no idea
what parents
think about things we ride

their back seats mow
their lawns carry
up and down driveways their

garbage cans for that
we get our rooms
and white jeans our records

and new horns and every
school day the walk
down Anderson

so one day
maybe we
grow up

+

girls live past
the park on the right
one has a dad who built

a swimming pool one
is buxom in the line up
for class photo girls

in the back row girls
in dresses girls whose names
you write *Brenda*

and *Joan*
Lisa Diane
Colleen

+

night comes
morning neighbour Mitchum
picks you up in his Olds

for a job in his warehouse
with working men (you neither *working*
nor *man*) talking *titties*

and *going home to hump the old*
lady in Ukrainian swear
all day you learn

4

rough games your voice
deepens your legs shoot
your jeans your sisters

can't believe that man
speaking from
your body

\+

the story goes
Eva got relieved of her
darkness back of Gardiner

easement (12-foot
right-of-way no
alleys in Hillsdale) running from

the park ease meant
play hide smoke spraypaint
who you are or

become you
and Eva dropping
acid on the floor

of a great sea a sign
says *My Cat*
Squirrelly Wants

Back Home Please
If You See Him
Do Call

+

In 1948, Bob Kramer — entrepreneur,
philanthropist, sportsman — purchased
the 600-acre McCallum-Hill

farm from Walter Hill and
heirs of the McCallum bros. In 1954
Kramer sold most of the land

back to McCallum-Hill.
The property was developed
into what is now

known as Hillsdale

1.1 Plaque at Kramer and Wascana

+

a time like this point out
philanthropism yes
what they did

for downtown how far
their name builds
time and land and letters

to/from the City
strong in the Roman
Catholic church how

could one criticize profit
works for all even me
in our shiny floors

blocks/lots
patios our L-
shapes our

steps going down
bedrooms our peacock
feather flags

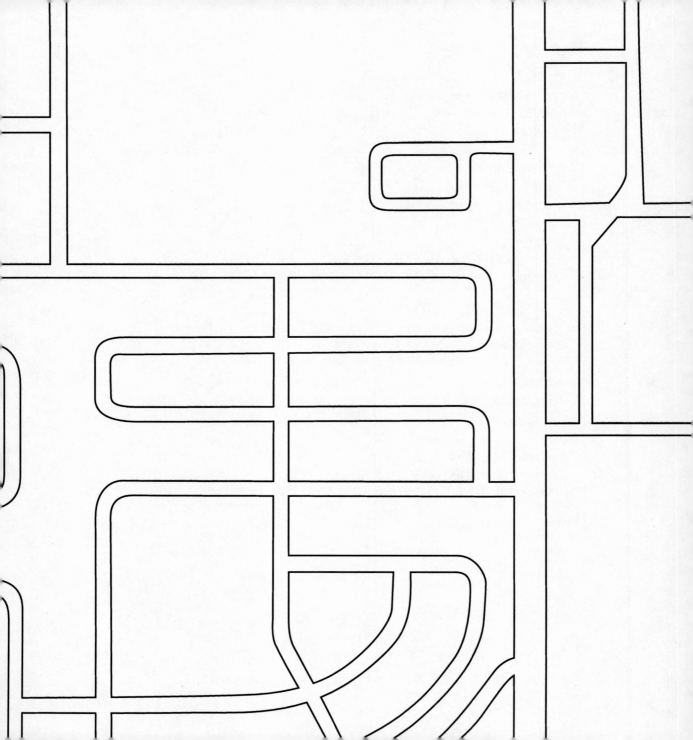

LAND FORMS

As always, one begins with the land.
— **SPIRO KOSTOF**, *The City Shaped: Urban Patterns and Meanings Through History*

+

proglacial lake

sedimentary basin

Precambrian basement

rumpus room

+

five hundred meters of late Mesozoic
earth that floor
so polyurethane my bedroom let's
follow it down get stuck in a word
gumbo

+

The City had our street draining to the middle. One neighbour got
after the City to do something about "Lake Langley," as she called it.
They came and repaired it a little, but I have a lake in front of my
place every time it rains.

+

earth becomes field

land becomes lot

city becomes house

room becomes boy

becomes latest worry

+

Frontier Life of the Future City (as found in the journal of Robert Sinton)

I homesteaded in 1882.

Many a morning I would drag a sheet over the dew. Wringing this into a pail, I procured enough water for immediate needs.

In the winter of 1882-83 the only fresh meat in Regina was buffalo meat brought in by the half-breeds.

This railroad construction camp was destined to become the capital of the Northwest Territories. I decided to locate here permanently.

After the rebellion by Louis Riel burst to flame, I met the mounted police and a band of volunteer soldiers returning from the battle of Duck Lake.

After the capture of Riel, I accompanied the Riel papers to Regina.

A Métis man guarded Riel's body in the basement of St. Mary's
church for two weeks after the hanging. I arrived with cart and
horse to haul the body to the station, St. Boniface train.

1906 I sold the ground on which the parliament building now stands
to McCallum-Hill, who sold a portion to the provincial government.
They used the rest for Hillsdale.

✚

Been measured been surveyed sub-
divided fitted with sidewalks (north
side only) been signed seen and ridden
seeded and pastured been a horse-girl's dream
Kramer's land and Sinton's and the CPR's
government of Canada's nobody's land
but people who wintered watered found fuel
north of here at the creek and brought down
buffalo gathered their bones heavy piles
by the tracks hauled east.

✚

drift undifferentiated

till

sand

sand and gravel

clay and silt

silt and sand

+

How do you do, Ravenscrag Formation!

+

Asphalt

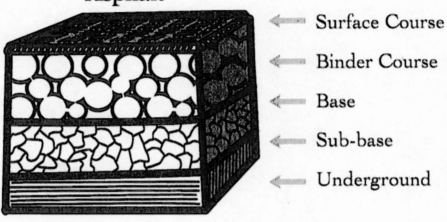

Surface Course

Binder Course

Base

Sub-base

Underground

1.2 Composition

+

Dad had the chance to buy the land where your house is for $30/acre in the 30s. He didn't want it — too much low ground, too much slough. He used to hunt on it, ducks.

+

Anderson the Premier
Bell the foreman in the City parks department
Bole the MLA
Bryant the lawyer
Calder the chooser of site of the Legislature
Cowan the dentist
Cross the Colonel
Darke the meat-seller and philanthropist
Davis the editor and the ambassador
Dunning the premier
Gardiner the premier
Haultain the Chief Justice
Hill the real estate developer
Jubilee the anniversary
Knowles the Anglican bishop
Kramer the principal and the land-owner
Lake the lieutenant-governor and effect of rain
Lamont the entrepreneur
Langley the MLA
Latta the author and commissioner of boy scouts
Laverendrye the fur trader and explorer
MacPherson the attorney-general
McNab the lieutenant-governor
McNiven the barrister
Martin the druggist and mayor, and the premier
Motherwell the homesteader
Munroe the minister of health
Newlands the lieutenant-governor
Parker the children's librarian and the lieutenant-governor
Parliament the federal institution
Patterson the premier and lieutenant-governor
Proctor the judge
Scott the mayor and the premier and the Library board member
Spence the member of Agriculture Hall of Fame
Turgeon the chief justice
Uhrich the physician and lieutenant-governor

1.3 Men Who Became Streets Laid on Land Developed by McCallum-Hill Who Bought it From R.A.Sinton Who Bought it From the CPR Whose Title to the Land Was Invented by the Government of Canada

+

pavement all humped and the trees (were
        not-trees) on mornings like this
                by the thousand since the last

glacier pulled
        away or is it
                light or a man

standing hero his eyes on
        time *can you*
                here me?

+

(Speaking For) The Equine Body

You can sense a horse
will startle at sight of a bird
(deer fox rabbit). Calm with voice
soothe with body. Horses are sure-

footed if you trust them.
Trot canter gallop walk all the gaits
up and down ditches. Unless they're
show horses they prefer

fun ride open field.
You and the sky just go
gallop gallop. Once
on Jenny my beloved mare (Arabian

still alive) I left
the corral never got
to the field. I'd bent to adjust
the stirrup reins in one hand not aware

of much except my foot. I remember
flying through the air (where
else) hitting the horse
ending at a hard word ground.

I heard horses I tried
crawling tried to yell
dusty very hot. When
the ambulance came they had to

slide me under the fence of the corral. I'd broken
toes and my collarbone before. Surgery
is great but they can't re-invent
what you used to be.

+

rain tones rain
        stones rain notes
                train roans the horse woman

keeping stones rain
        where it comes from or
                lands north of 23rd

what I wake to
        no hurry to
                do this it'll rain all day

+

Driving out of town to
        Moose Jaw today I see land
                only a few lots left! I see

future home of *RK Moving*
        and Storage. Developers
                on City Council make deals

re: fields *where we used to run*
        our hotrods.[1] I see 1956
                annexation *reach*

just across the road from our place[2] see
　　　　　　　　through my windows the long story
　　　　　　　　　　　　　　land is the document (airy)

legend of land. Level
　　　　　　　　or not here I come now
　　　　　　　　　　　　　　entering. I imagine

a suburb[3] *first right first left*
　　　　　　　　first right first left
　　　　　　　　　　　　　　second from the end

on the right.[4] I see land
　　　　　　　　attached to my hand by
　　　　　　　　　　　　　　a survey stick a boy's time

how he lands it.

✚

history in Hillsdale? hell
my own history is longer

```
  T     T     T     T     T
  R     R     R     R     R
TREESTREETREESTREESTREETS
  E     E     E     E     E
  T     T     T     T     T
  R     R     R     R     R
TREESTREETREESTREESTREETS
  E     E     E     E     E
  T     T     T     T     T
  R     R     R     R     R
  E     E     E     E     E
TREESTREETREESTREESTREETS
  S     S     S     S     S
  T     T     T     T     T
  R     R     R     R     R
  E     E     E     E     E
TREESTREETREESTREESTREETS
  S     S     S     S     S
  T     T     T     T     T
  R     R     R     R     R
  E     E     E     E     E
TREESTREETREESTREESTREETS
  T     T     T     T     T
  S     S.    S     S     S
```

1.4 Urban Design, The Grid System: Straight Through Anywhere

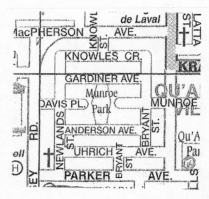

1.5 Urban Design, Hillsdale 1955: Peripheral Location, Asymmetric Pattern of Curved Streets, Through-traffic at Perimeter, Low Density, Car Culture Assumed, Architectural Uniformity, Easier Access to Long-term Low-interest Loans (thanks to the CMHC)

1.6 Early Hillsdale, looking west over McVeety School

your space looks familiar
how schoolish your emptiness
newly fenced how wide

the goodness of Jubilee avenue how farmed off
the edges how close your Safeway
un-dense your destiny how one-sided

sidewalks how emptying
your moving van open your fields
ex your farm lined up

you huddle there
building what is good for you and
the others good

+

Hillsdale "A"	1955	Plan No. FT 1642
Hillsdale "B"	1956	Plan No. FN 2102
Hillsdale "C"	1957	Plan No. FV 2273
Hillsdale "D"	1957	Plan No. FZ 2501
Hillsdale "E"	1958	Plan No. GE 191
Hillsdale "F"	1959	Plan No. 59R02162
Hillsdale "G"	1961	Plan No. 61R06750

1.7 For These Be the Subdivisions of Hillsdale

+

built with cars in
mind in motion in and out
the hearts of neighbourhood cells
80 feet wide (the perimeter
roads) 50 feet the interior

Blues Here
House of the Surprising Sun
I Just Wanna Want You
The Ballad of Sal Mineo
Parliament Chill
Darke Meat
Ground Around Midnight
Older But Deeper
(Sister #1's) Long White Veil
GTO Calcutta
Suburb'n Fuse

1.8 Playlist of The Sediments, a Deep Rock Band, Who Played Northwest of Moose Jaw to East of Here (Opening act: Raven's Crag)

Good-bye ancient Lake Regina!

THE ONE NEW

A broken oar
is found by the searching waters.
W.C. WILLIAMS, *Paterson, Book Three*

Sister 2 and Mom find
        the house *she had brochures*
                spread out on the bed at the Drake

Hotel (Dad away at
        summer school) the wide
                plain open only a neighbour's house

and holes Dad wanted garage
        Mom fireplace he tells her over
                the phone *Well you buy*

the house and she does (no garage
        no fireplace) the one new
                house they'd ever own

that first year
        land answers to
                mud all around

+

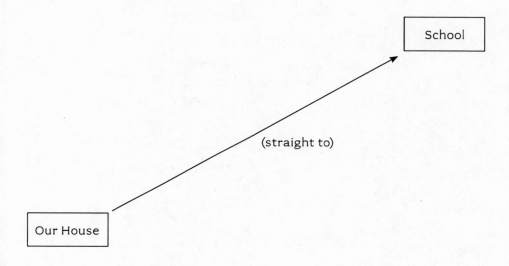

1.9 Before the Rest of the Houses Were Built

+

Survey sticks I play with
        here I am measuring
                stick as sword jet

machete stick an old
        man stick boat don't need
                shovel when I got stick-all.

Pull loose a stick
        at night where they plan
                to dig. Result? a house

out of line. Stick flag
                stick rifle bat spear stick
                                my nose in a culvert catch

Sister 3 smoking cigars stick hammer
                stick gong (she's
                                sick for a week I'm

stick a whole
                summer) I play with
                                what to stick to.

+

Sisters, Their Drain Age

All night all day
we mop in shifts
mop and stay up

make toast the builder
screwed up plain
and simple the house

too low grading poor
Mom and Dad away wouldn't
you know it

five feet of water!
Vestner comes over and tells us
our sump pump has cemented in

exactly what he says "cemented in"
the piano is floating! Mom's Kenmore
sinks your precious pool table

bobs against the fake
mahogany my toybox
is lost and all our prom

dresses (well I didn't have
a prom dress) dad's army
uniform my first wedding dress

+

           I lay
                in the lower bedroom rear of the house and claimed it
hardwood in hot sun claimed it
             lay down on the hardwood August '61
       or laid down?
           Dad would correct me but didn't
      when I lay there
         no lie
my bedroom for ten years
             always worried so
      shy I
        lay/lie
       low

+

new corners gleam
        concrete lays bright
                windows the siding fresh

beige carpets softsteps
        no one ever took but
                builders and Mom and Sister 2

when they viewed
        the house and kids when
                the basement was dug

me the first
        boy to lie here
                the first boy I like that

+

A Boy's Room 1962

> The private bedroom, a Georgian innovation for a growing inner life
> and the need to express this in physical ways.
> — **WITOLD RYBCZYNSKI**, *Home, A Short History of An Idea*

ENTER HERE

i. Light a south window.

ii. The Finn kid next door Catholic kid
     red hair shoots baskets
     bouncing.[5]

iii. Ledge along two walls five
      feet up a Sopwith Camel and
      HMCS Regina.

iv. 12-volume set of *Britannica Junior*
     I read I don't know why.

v. Transistor radio vinyl case I hear
    Oklahoma's hot.

vi. Wooden desk what I know of
     office surplus and *thump*
     thump it's Finn again.

vii. Remington portable black
      case lid hook from
      the hinges and close.

viii.   Trombone music stand noon
         I practice.
         The Finn kid's at school.

   ix.   Bi-fold closet white jeans
                        Mr. Charles shirts
          Mad magazines.

    x.   Pennants felt but not
          remembered Vernon
          Winnipeg Minot.

    EXIT HERE

+

What Sisters Have to Say

On that phone nook near the front door:
 I didn't get to use it much because this one [Sister 2] was on the phone
 constantly, her head down like this, talking on the phone for hours.

On furniture:
 Mom and Dad won pictures and a vase, nice stereo we use a lot, the
 couch and the mirror I still have. They won a swivel rocker, coffee and end
 tables — won a full room of furniture, all of it, in a Lions Club draw.

On What Dad Wants:
 They added swinging doors, saloon doors. Dad said he hated to walk
 in the front door and see the kitchen.[6]

On Getting Mom an Automatic Dishwasher:

*"I have dishwashers," Mom would say. My turn was the morning.
She'd have her coffee, one gulp left, and she'd go down to
throw some laundry in. I'd clean her cup. She'd come up and say
"Where's my coffee?" I'd say, "There was hardly any left. I dumped
it out," and she'd say "I had my mouth set for that last mouthful."
I never knew what she meant, but now I sure do.*

On Having Your Own Bed in a Brand New Room:

*I got to pick the curtains and the bedspread. Twin beds, I thought I'd
found heaven.*

On Getting to Sleep:

*My hair in curlers, I hear Sister 2's friends on the stairs doing
"Romeo, Romeo, wherefore art thou?" I come out of our bedroom in
my curlers and give them a blast: "Wherefore art thou? Wherefore
%&*)&^*&%^*&$." A real bitch, you know.*

On Mom's Devotion to Old Machines:

*When we first moved, she kept the wringer-washer. Then she got a
Kenmore washer and dryer. Oh boy, she was beside herself.*

✚

I'm a newborn calf
                 my father's arm around me
                               on the couch how badly
he wants to love
                 I'm saying this fifty
                            years later all I knew

at the time of this man
            unsparing (a word just now
                        I looked up) all I knew

were small things
            index cards / shirt pocket
                        ballpoint pen he'd watch

if you borrowed and books
            all around yes thanks dad
                        for Dickens and Louis L'Amour

+

What do you want?
            Football helmet.

Are you sure you want a football helmet?
                        Yes.

Three-speed bike?
            Yes.

Brand new silver-plated trombone left on the steps where you'll find it?
                        I prefer the gold.

+

that door lids my space I'm
            used to yellow dresser
                        bi-fold closet

window the back yard
        leads window to
                door my brain

escapes that room
        I enter and mom
                to clean and dad

to check homework thanks
        room for fears and longings I'll never be
                a man without

+

we aren't allowed to eat
        in front of the tv
                yet we eat "tv dinners"

mashed potatoes peas and carrots
        corn turkey or Swiss steak
                fruit salad I rather like them

mom makes real ones weeks
        she's curling gets dad
                to warm them up

the Schmidts built a bomb shelter
        I don't know what they eat in there
                tv dinners I suppose

You Hear Things in Neighbourhoods

you hear of suburbs in Don Mills
                and Winnipeg that's why
                                we need one here your uncle pretends

he can't hear your aunt you hear
                depression at the NW corner
                        of Calder *not just the gutter but*

the whole damn street [7] you hear Hill
                of McCallum-Hill sat on City Council
                        around the time the Master Plan

for Hillsdale was approved a*nd did you know*
                he hired the City Manager
                        as development head of McCallum-Hill! [8]

you hear new names for streets Boy Bay
                Moon Crescent you hear
                        everybody's do-oo-ing a

brand new dance
                now you hear
                      her

Cake contest at the Exhibition Grounds turns
sticky when Pauline K. accuses
winner Helen Clawrence of icing
her way to top prize.

1.10 The Contest

I walk Eva north
            to Hillsdale Sunday
                        afternoon supposed to be

warm wind today we've been
            to Sherry's party *Please*
                        Please Me I'm leaving

with Eva don't want to be
            out in that wind alone I reach
                        across oops don't get my

fantasy steaming I didn't
               hold hands ask her out I said
                        how about this wind

blowing past the school left
               on Newlands a block
                        to make my move

what move suppose
               I press against her parka
                        to parka pull our hands

close to our faces oops
               I love to say
                        this happens

+

A Boy's Dream 1961

I have woken up before
               a room first light first ten words
                        tremor-familiar bones

Mom upstairs in that wide
               kitchen she never says
                        she loves Sister 3 rode the bus

downtown yesterday for fries
               and a Coke she and Barb went straight
                        to the rink afterwards though Dad said

not to *that man who waters ice*
    I don't want you near him he's
        harmless Sister 3 says old

that's all with a fire that's all
    she and Barb melt
       their vinyl purses to the stove

a pause and I find a great ship
    in Wascana lake I haul water
       by the glassful till it floats

it never floats
    I never dream
      long enough

+

Sister 2 is hosting Sorority initiation, Stigma Lamborghini Chai.
She's the President. We're told not to set foot downstairs.
"Especially you" [to me]. "I don't want any of your comedy routines."

She says to mom "Have you got any candles, I'd like to light some
candles". All we have is the kind you use for insects, citronella.
She says "I'll take them."

Mom and I are on the floor laughing because we can smell this citronella.

No bugs at that party.

Snow Time (Like the Present)

First Wicked Sister:
All he had to do was take out the garbage.

Second Wicked Sister:
I thought there was one other thing.

Third Wicked Sister:
That was it, sisters. That was it.

Every winter from then to now I shovel while Sisters preen — tub
of toenail polish, nail files, panic of split ends. That's them on their
telephone, playing their LPs, dreaming of their boyfriends' cars.

All day I shovel, high as a boy can reach, higher, columns (call 'em walls)
of snow, nothing beyond but more of it. Whoever I'll be starts here,
my one-boy campaign. For all the Sisters in Hillsdale the driveway
must be cleared.

"Suppertime," mother calls, the light thin, a brief afternoon. I shovel
on — no egg-tomato casserole for me. Warm in the kitchen, Sisters
pick at their food, argue who is to wash who to dry. Maidens do whine,
I guess. A cold wind runs against my stooping, stupid back, my doomed-
grey parka, fur hood. Snowcliffs rise ever-steeper.

Through the long night I shovel that mad glow. I pause a moment, the
snow does not. I shovel, re-shovel. Down flutters snow. In their bright
rooms, baby-dolls and nighties, perms, the three Sisters turn in their
sleep, sigh.

By morning, that dome of snowy light far overhead, my shovel has worn to a one-inch blade which, with one titanic cast of snow, falls loose at my feet, first dusted then buried by continuing passions of snow. With a three-foot shaft an inch in diameter I shovel on. Hours later I climb the snowcliff to peer down to the house, its curtains drawn, windows frosted, furls of smoke idling from the chimney, yes, and dim strains of pop tunes. I burrow in and rest a while.

Come spring, the snow has melted and laid me gently on the sidewalk next to our Plymouth. Mother calls from the front step. *Come in for some hot tomato soup, son.* I lift myself, clap ice fragments from my parka and step inside.

Sisters 1, 2 and 3 stand there next to the telephone nook, their hair in rollers. *Look at him,* they say, *the lazy slug.*

+

Imagine a Story [9]

Dad said *revolver.* I said
        What do you mean? (I'd watched
               Have Gun Will Travel that very night).

Dad looked at Mom. She got up
        left the room. *Well* Dad said
                looking like he had to declare

a disease. *I found a revolver*
        out back, we were digging a hole
                Bob Mitchum and me for the fence.

He left silence. Here was
        my chance. *Can I see it?* I said.
                Sorry, can't do that. I felt as if I'd

jabbed my palm on a broken stick.
        What do you mean? Why not?
                and now as I tell this I can't be sure

what a man like him would have said
        except *I chucked it away.* I saw
                him stir, about to get up.

The moment of usual vanishing was
        at hand. *Chucked it away*
                where? I damn near broke the metal

strip round the kitchen table. Dad looked
        a good five seconds and nodded
                toward the door and said

Been down to the lake lately? Oh
        for God's sake I heard
                Mom from the living room say.

Mrs. Shippi, 10 Haultain, enquires regarding the possibility of a bus shelter on Scott Street.

Numerous complainants: sidewalk and road at Calder Crescent and Jubilee Avenue.

Mr. E.Sullivan at 1405 McPherson brings to my attention the condition of the curb in front of his house.

A resident complains about the length of time the lights are kept on at the tennis courts at LeBoldus High School. In fall no one plays after dark because of cold. Turn the lights off!

Mr. Birdless, 46 Massey, complains that the cleaning of Balfour Arena with a tractor early in the morning makes sleep impossible.

Mrs. Silvermore at 1208 Jubilee complains about the condition of the sidewalk in front of her home.

1.11 The Candidate's Issues

+

One month into this
        "Hillsdale" here I am
                across from a Psychologist

in the School Nurse office with no
        idea why the man says *If it were two*
                hours later it would be half as long

to midnight as it would be
        one hour later what time
                is it now? and *pear is to*

apple as potato is to?
        I don't know afterwards
                he looks at me I can hear

my classmates play marbles
        outside he'd been worried
                there for a minute he says

(I do remember
        a long pause) over-all
                satisfactory I'd do

grades five and six
        in a single year
                I'm younger from then on

+

Neal and Barry
          every day the way to school
               left on Newlands or

right Neal and Barry
          arms crossed
               stand there

how scared are you today?

+

Massey Schoolyard Song of World Affairs c. 1961
(to tune of Colonel Bogey March)

Hitler
had only one big ball

Stalin
had two but they were small

Himmler
had something similar

and Khrushchev
has no balls
at all

+

In the free world of Hillsdale
                an air raid siren stands sixty feet
                                high up poles in the southeast

corner of Massey schoolyard
                in case of invasion from Russia from
                                the night just done from neighbouring

schools with twins who argue
                and an English kid
                                the whole English invasion

+

        girls wore dresses
                        boys tab collars
        white jeans and socks
                        alpaca sweaters
        I wrote my *girlfriend*
                (in my scribbler) *is Brenda Brown*
oh my god she was standing
                right there reading the first
        girl I'd loved reading

✚

I must have been a boy
        many years ago to mount
                on my wall a peacock feather

a woman who knew things
        gave me she knew
                a bird's cry in the olive tree

at dusk when the fox
        comes out she's in the Gulf Islands now
                having lost something or other

on an acid trip in Toronto
        does it matter how
                long ago this was?

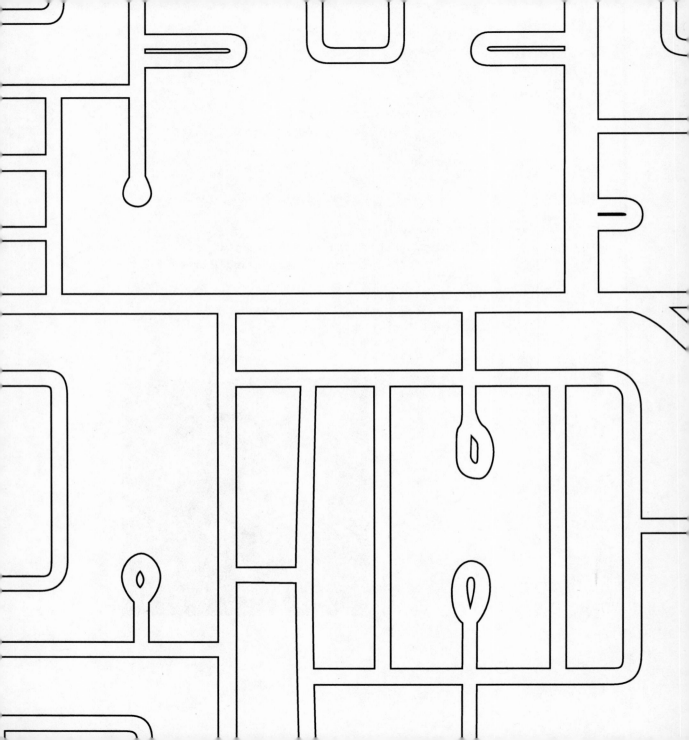

FLO

history being in me is my story
— **bp** NICHOL *The Martyrology* Book 1

+

You think back a bit.

We moved in '56 or '57 one or the other, I'm going by memory.
Lorne was transferred. We had to pick up and go.

Our house on McNab was the end of everything. One night our first
winter in the house a young girl came crying to our door. She'd been
raped out in that field behind us. It was dark and she was so scared.

Other than that McNab treated us well.

+

Counting the crescent and up to Jubilee — 40 children, I was counting
last night. Soon as someone moved in you'd have a coffee party and
get to meet them all, you know, coffee party once a month at least.
A few years later we'd have going away parties.

The kids got us together, they made friends so fast. You didn't need
entertainment for children. They just played.

We told the kids not to go as far as the lake but they often came home
with wet pants. You knew darned well where they'd been. It was a worry
because of the geese. Vicious! They were braver then.

My youngest daughter was five when she took the bus to kindergarten.
By herself. And you didn't worry.

Push the kids out the door, let them walk to school!

+

Someone would phone and say "Flo, you going to be home? I'm tied up longer than I thought at the doctor's. Can the kids come to your place after school?" This kind of stuff you just did. You didn't think about it.

We had a two-table bridge club for years and years and we joined the Lioness Club and the Catholic Women's League. We'd have baby showers, we'd have bridal showers, we'd have coffee. Somebody would get the idea to have everyone over this morning and away you'd go.

A group of us got together to hold services at the Wascana Rehab in the auditorium there. Lorne and I were charter members. I'm afraid I'm not very faithful anymore.

Mixed curling every second Saturday night. We'd curl, we'd come back for this enormous spread of food — don't know why we thought we needed so much food when we'd already eaten supper.

Why, with no back alleys in this new subdivision, we have to leave our garbage out front. Imagine!

At first the only trees were the ones we'd left in Battleford. You can't walk now without trees. Look, Mrs. Klipp planted a weeping birch in the front, middle of the lawn. She didn't like it or the insects did, it died.

At our place Lombardy poplars in the backyard were nice but in spring no leaves came out. The nursery guy said "Put in some male poplars. They'll grow fast and won't shed". He sold us three male poplars. I don't know how you could tell the difference. They grew so tall after 30 years we began to worry about one of them falling on us. Lorne cut them down. That was this century, I guess.

The poplars right now, a lot of them dying. After 30-35 years they go downhill. Once that happens the insects or diseases conditional to that tree take hold, you know? The cankers and that kind of thing.

For our first anniversary Lorne's parents gave us a Colorado green spruce seedling. We argued over where to put it. Friends brought us two beautiful honeysuckle for the back yard, about three feet tall, brought them in the trunk of their Dodge. Maybe it wasn't honeysuckle.

Yes at one time Hillsdale was big into the weeping birch but they all succumbed.

+

*You get a rainy day around the government buildings and the worms get
trapped in the gutter. Lorne picked up a pail of these earthworms and seeded
our place. He had the idea they'd break down the gumbo. Of course the
earthworms multiplied and moved out into the neighbourhood.*

*The back yard was filled with construction garbage. It eventually cleared out and
we could plant the back to grass. We got wheelbarrows of earth from out in the
field and put it in the trenches for our vegetables and things. But it was blowdirt,
absolutely no goodness in it. Our vegetables were not great that first year.*

*Finally we brought in topsoil to get the grass started. Just when we got the grass
into that very sensitive stage, the City rationed water. We all used to cheat at
night — you had to, to save the grass. I heard the police came out and listened
for hoses at night. We were careful, we didn't want to end up in court.*

*We put in our lawn after I dug the potatoes and have not changed lawn since.
Everyone else has changed their lawns two or three times.*

+

*You want to put up a garage, City tree is in the way. You want to cut it down,
City ordinance says you can't.*

*So you can't take down the City tree, and the City doesn't want to either. Some
say "To hell with you" and cement or asphalt around the tree.*

*Well they've sentenced the tree to death. No root surface left at all. Then there's
a big fight, a court case.*

Realtors buy houses in this area and rent them out. I don't like that.

Young families are moving in again. Old families move or die, one of the two. I don't even know names of people next door.

The young families are doing renovations because it's affordable. A lot of older people haven't done diddly and that's a shame. Now people whose houses aren't in very good shape can flip them for $300,000. The buyer has to spend a hundred thousand renovating.

Children had to stay on the sidewalk in the '50s, they couldn't play on the street. Assuming there was a sidewalk, assuming there was a street. The little people that live here now, they're all over the place. You really have to watch when you're backing up.

I spoke to a young fellow down the street and said we should throw another block party and he agreed. Even just the two of us sitting outside on a nice day having a beverage.

Viv Schmidt and I were neighbours for 51 years, until a year ago July. Friends all those years. I sure miss her.

+

So much water one year we couldn't drive cars. I phoned two neighbours and asked them each to phone two neighbours to ask City Hall when they would come and open the drains. The City said, "Couldn't someone go out there and open them?" I said, "Which one of us 80-year-old people would you like to do it?" The man who used to do it died.

I was comfortable in that house for 52 years. When Lorne passed away it was just too much. I gave up on the house, sold it in one day.

I had a garden always. I just couldn't do it anymore.

They're all dead now. Mr. Lloyd is in Wascana Rehab but you might talk to him. He's got a good mind still.

✚

Here's a story about the little girl next door who turned out not so little. Victoria loved Elvis Presley. She had her own record player and all the Elvis records. She knew how to work it and everything. We all thought wow, she's really sophisticated.

She was more mature, physically, for her age. Ahead of my girls in interest in boys and that sort of thing. Later she got involved with a fellow from a different area and got pregnant. I remember sitting in the living room with daughter #1, Susan. She said "Well, I can't believe it. I wouldn't touch sex with a ten-foot pole." I looked at her and said "Well, don't be too hasty."

It was true Victoria would sneak in and out of the window of her house, right by our driveway. It was a bit of a drop from the window to the ground.

But the kids sure had fun. That about says it all when you're a kid. Yes, what else could you say.

Everyone was our age, Lorne's and mine. All starting and had young children and all had to get rubber boots.

We'd throw a block party in summer, set up barbecues on the driveway we shared with the Spilliams. People brought their own food. It was great getting to know our neighbours a bit. Lots of kids, lots of drinks spilled.

Spilliams tore their fence down and wanted us to tear ours down. They couldn't see any sense in the fence. I would have torn it down but Lorne didn't want to.

We had a boxer named Daisy. You know, boxers are strong. We put up a fence and a wire over top and she jumped over that. We put a wire a foot higher and she jumped over that. One Sunday she jumped down the street where the ladies in their hats and white gloves were going to church. Daisy jumped into the back seat of the car with them all. The ladies were very nice about it.

I don't think I've told you very much.

THE TRAVELLER'S REPLY

By its nature, the metropolis provides what otherwise could
be given only by traveling: namely, the strange.
— **JANE JACOBS**, *The Death and Life of Great American Cities*

+

'61: came back: '95

no why

yes why!

:chance / choice

I and my ex-wife made

hers a house

a block from

our house in '61

+

Notes, a Not-book[10]

I am not buried in trees.
I am not the pelicans swans geese beyond no I am not that.
I do not walk tethered to dogs.
I am not precarious over time.
I am not Maureen Martin the '59 Exhibition Wheat Queen posing with the Mayor.
Gideon of Scotland Yard playing at the Rex on 11th not that.
Not the fragment entirely.
I am not released like hounds from a Jeep on Uhrich.

I am not opposed to stealing my own hair — see cache July 2009.
I am not *an ordinary man gazing at a scene becom[ing]*
aware of what's before him[11] certainly I'm not that.
I am not a permanent dwelling.
I do not smoke or drink or swear I do not smoke.
I do not hold to your snickers (try me later about your knickers).
I am not the search for the poem's own language.
I do not want to be Miles Davis.
But two minutes after recess I want the seat of the swing to stay warm.
I am not alive in my father's house.
I am not hand-drawn.
I take no wow of silence.

+

the traveller helps himself
                to past or present
                                by accident people say

they have nothing to say
                the traveller becomes
                                a boy the boy replays

trauma from '62
                he looks like walking
                                his layers ache

everywhere he puts his foot
                his foot's been
                                not counting the easement

inside Knowles the difference
 from then to now is
  fifty years give or take *trees*

how big? I brought seedlings
 *home on Arbor Day w*here Bryant
  meets Anderson

Anderson meets Bryant
 tired of memory he'd rather
  just see

✚

Dear Roberts Plaza Resistance Committee,

your story or my
                story for you is
                                Roberts wanted to build

three more *and* a string
                of low-rises between
                                you and the lake you all paid

a hundred bucks for
                a lawyer who like you
                                moved here to avoid

high-density
                looking down on
                                what you were doing and worse

the Plaza blocked your ramble
                round the lake way to win
                                injunctions delays

way to turn media *blitz*
                to *bliss* way to stop
                                the buggers cold

✚

(for Flo and Lorne)

Is it true you found dirt back
                of your first and only married home?
                                First time saying *blowdirt?*

and *Sod's just for rich folks?*
                    Children trying to get out
                                        the bathroom window of a burning

house on Martin did I get that right?
                    Did neighbours drive over or through your
                                        ornamental crab?

How is it Margie came along
                    after you moved
                                        your bedroom closer to birds?

Did Margie disappear one afternoon?
                    You looked down the manhole at McNab
                                        and Jubilee. What's down there?

Did Margie want the sandbox in the back and a wooden fence?
                    This Margie does she
                                        care for you now?

+

Same time the traveller shot exposed rebar
at 29 Munroe he heard his knee.
In the physiotherapist office he circled
kneeling to photograph

as *activity I cannot do.*
She felt his meniscus and assigned
three sets of Knee Dogs (five reps) and said
come back see me in a week.

+

Smart Funny Stacked and Likes to Sing

(for Eva)

Years I've had one eye on you *two.*

Hours per day of flat-out yearn *twenty-three.*

Chance you'd kiss me *lower than zero.*

You like me but not the way

you save for Rob

Bruce or Gary. I ask you to grad

you say *Thank you*
                  for asking but
                                   I'm already going with Rob

Bruce or Gary.
                  Bike ahead twenty years
                                two of us over coffee. *I knew*

nothing else but wanting you.
                  You look at me tender
                                as wind when it's tender

as June afternoons *Oh Gerry —*
                  if I'd only known
                                I'd love to have been with you.

The spruce buds
                  are new that's what reminds me
                                what we do to ourselves.

+

I recommend the duck [12]
                  corner of Bryant
                                and Munroe duck and Ford turning

slowest duck ever to cross
                  Munroe the duck sips a puddle
                                walks the lawn at 106

memory-sure
                  I recommend
                                seeing it all now

✚

well the knee bone connected to the
thigh bone
      the thigh bone connected to the
hip bone
    the hip bone connected to the
back bone
     the back bone connected to the
head bone
     the head bone connected to the
sky bone
    the sky bone connected to the
rain bone
     the rain bone connected to the
street bone
      the street bone connected to the
foot bone
     the foot bone connected to the
leg bone
     the leg bone connected to the
knee bone and oh can't
        the traveller
          feel it.

+

motorist collides with deer
                last week she drives
                          her Bonneville gift from her father
         east

on 23rd does not
             sustain injury the deer as far
                      as conservation agents can detect

will live of the Bonneville
             no more is seen but the key
                    in her armoire gift from her mother
        with

barrettes and so on the wild
            finds traffic the farmers
                  plant in spring

the animals will come
           not much to be but wary.
                  Wary? I <u>was</u>

says a girl in a mirror
             gift from her aunt *how about*
                  more signs more

warning a picture of
           moose or coyote crossing 23rd
                  in the foreground my Bonneville

windows down pony-tail a No
          to Wildlife gal if you don't mind
                I <u>was</u> wary

compared to the deer.

+

July night a man
    works a '55 Olds 88 *runs great I get*
        4 in the city 7 on the highway

what a beauty his '68
    Bonneville ambulance that drove
       all over Moose Jaw *dandy*

for bush parties get a lot
    of people in there good hobby?
       good for driving me crazy

+

Sunrise, a Hillsdally: Be Yonder

after sunrise Hillsdalians
    emerge supposed to be
       hot today beyond

morning beyond wind
    running hollow in Hillsdale
       they die elsewhere a man

tips ashes of his wife into
    petunias under the picture
       window and gives

the house to her sister
                    who'd nursed her
                                        the sister gives it to

her son who doesn't
                    look after it but
                                        some day might

+

traveller glimpses
                    poplar gleams further east
                                        an elm reads *older*

+

after high school Hillsdale
                    boys *went out*
                                        to the railroad [13] Bill's dad

long-time CPR
                    man every summer said
                                        get me a crew soon

a Dodge left town with four
                    Hillsdale boys westbound
                                        thirty-five or forty

years some of them worked
                    the mountains full
                                        of retired Hillsdale boys

70

(for T. and the Kenton 'bones)

       No lyric poems in Hillsdale but light
                flickers longer and "Here's
                                That Rainy Day" *Scott LaFaro*

*   flickered just a moment more himself*
*   beyond that Village Vanguard date*
                        is the kind of thing you'd say

     playing Bill Evans
              or the Kenton band *Cuban Fire!*
                      driving that Chevy east

as you said you would.

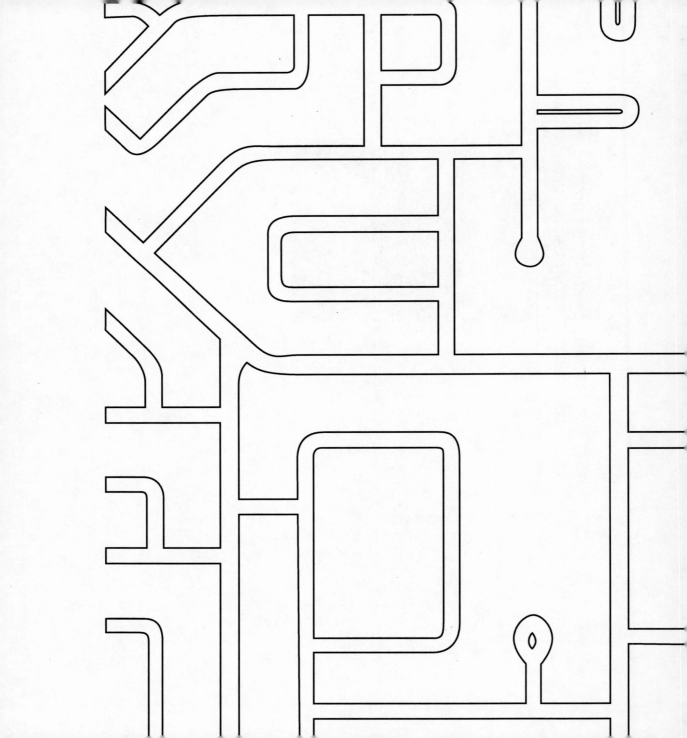

STREETPIECES

If a street leads to a road you are heading out of town.
If a road turns into a street you are heading into town. . . .
The best streets urge you to stay; the road is an endless
incentive to leave.

— **JOEL MEYEROWITZ**, *Creating a Sense of Place*

+

Uhrich Streetpiece: Rising

Uhrich rises east to west
lesson one for today: time
means landscape
rising roots and heaves.

A man releases long-legged hounds
from the rear of his Jeep. The corner
of Bryant rises to curbs. *Flatten
and lift* mean *sidewalk.*

From the heart of your own attention rise.
Picture dips in the road. On Uhrich
they clip their radical hedge to knee-high
leaves the size of guitar picks and branches

thick as thumbs. Could be Logan who planted
in '60 or so could be Moon
the tenor player but he lived
further down on Uhrich there lower.

+

Turgeon Streetpiece: Hair Piece

He pays ten dollars plus tip
for his hairsnip and hides
in Turgeon Crescent for the post-
haircut tremor. Today for some reason he stole

a lock of his hair from the nylon
cape Allison of Ultracuts
covered him with. It's hot on Turgeon.
He rubs his head. Shavings

from her eighth-inch guide sift free.
He'd loaded a thimble-sized thatch
of hair into his hanky *for the street
piece on Turgeon* don't ask him why.

It's hot enough on Turgeon to jog
renovate your home in ask the City to ease
zoning bylaw 620
so at #37

they can legally build that new garage.
He carries on this way until his hair
he'd set on the dash scatters
ps from *snip*. Soon he's hairless as stone

edging the driveway of #40
or SCHOOL ZONE sign or shadow
gaps of light wear. Turgeon grows
hairless could hair less.

+

Scott Streetpiece: Wanting Joe Tims

*When Hillsdale was being developed the usual time frames for
homes was less than 6 months from start to finish. You could
reasonably assume that if a permit were issued in July 1956 the
home would have been finished by year end or shortly thereafter.*

Want the oldest
house in Hillsdale the Tims
bungalow 6 Scott stucco blinds
lowered a morning sun.

Want everything to matter
breeze sidewalk the #4 northbound
10:00 original curb in shadow
once the trees grew.

Want to care for what you see and so
see a SaskPower meter guy
call out (watching
out) for dogs. Child *Bird*

dead bird mother *I know I know.*
Want to find on Scott
up a new front step
Joe Tims.

+

Parliament Streetpiece: Bike Me

Back and forth past her house five of seven days
for a glimpse of her brushing her hair.

If I found her helping her brother wash the car
I felt cleaner myself.

If she rode toward me on her Laura-spin 50
I saw socks white sleeveless blouse jeans.

If she spoke
I heard wheels

in my mind and hit the brakes.
Or lilacs.

+

Parker Ave Streetpiece: Left

At my
old school
where
Sister 1 taught
and my
kids went
and my
daughter's
husband
went and
we all
played my
pals and
I heading
home to
the Three
Stooges
after school
here about place Bill's at left turn left at Bill's place about here.

+

Newlands Streetpiece: A Block or So

Two boys park their faded
Datsun behind the traveller
on Newlands this morning no rush
to get to school. They talk

laugh open the trunk fiddle with
backpacks their Tim Hortons beverage
wait for each other. The traveller
rolls the window down dogs bark

a garbage truck. Drizzly raw
the language of this morning
no land like new lands a block
or so from where he used to be.

+

Munroe Streetpiece: 1968

Seen from Apollo 8 the 2.59
acres off Munroe look pale green
to astronaut Frank Borman who sees
the sidewalk crossing the park *essentially*

gray like dirty sand. Ten times
they orbit once for every pass
my buddy Ken intercepts
from his dark deep

safety position. He watches
my eyes. By the time the ball
leaves my hand he's read its path
237 thousand miles below the astronauts

heading for the dark side. I like
the way the guy knows
how to beat you.
He picked off another one

Borman says passing the camera
to Lovell. That damn Ken
his Sea of Interception
his big year.

+

Motherwell Streetpiece: Mother Swell

3:00 bell of McVeety School.
As for mothers well the houses were theirs
the matrilineal compound that was
Hillsdale by day although by '57
the older children went to school at least.

> *Our entertainment was right here, right on*
> *this little corner. The ladies just went*
> *back and forth for tea in the afternoon*
> *while the kids played. It was pretty simple*
> *when we couldn't afford babysitters.*

As for mothers well they drove by Roberts
Plaza every Thursday to curl. They wore
stirrup pants and leather curling boots and
sweaters they'd knitted and scarves and felt hats
and curling pins they later gave away.

> All day there was a lot to do. Get flowers
> in, the lawn in, and then the kids would come
> home for lunch. After school you ran around.
> One would go swimming the other would go
> to piano then the other way around.

A warm stretch in early November time
to gather leaves once more with brooms, stiff rakes
lawnmowers and deep plastic bags, the lawns
still green under their rakes. They had few leaves
(few trees!) on Motherwell in '56.

> The City gave each schoolchild a tree.
> My daughter came home crying all the kids
> had great big trees hers was tiny. I said
> we'd care for it and it would grow bigger
> than the rest. You should see it out there now.

As for mothers well some planted potatoes
to break up the gumbo add nitrogen
to the soil. *They laughed when I planted
potatoes our first year* said Mrs. Ache
until they saw my harvest that autumn.

All I did was wash clothes. Oh the mud.
First we put cardboard down then scraps of wood.
Of course the kids would never stay on them.
You'd hear "So-and-so is stuck in the mud."
You'd have to go and pull the poor kid out.

They feel the warmth of sun on Motherwell
checking every few minutes to see if
it'll still be around in fifty years
for mothers in their chairs they never leave
sun till their time is done and then *oh well*

We had our yards to do our lives to make.
We loved the house, never wanted to move.
What did we hope for? I really don't know.
Just life I guess. I always felt my life
was far better than any I deserved.

+

McNiven Streetpiece: Reached

He sees his breath says his breath
reached (for) McNiven found the frost
scape of leaves and cars including
his own parked in front of the piano

teacher's house. None of that needs
finding nor do geese the students
walking through blue sky elms
near empty now the mighty red

hydrant a Darke look:
seniors home that used to be
easement that used to be
McNiven school empty northeast.

Looking for goalposts a boy makes
animal noises hat with floppy ears.
Mom smiles walks ahead stops
as the traveller does now looking back.

+

McNab Streetpiece: *deeply attached to hope* [14]

He parks it as thin black
car near the corner
facing north. A woman

rakes *making room*
for my neighbours' leaves. She points
across the street. *What are you gonna do?*

He walks the deep ache his left
knee presents. He hopes in black
and white manhole topping

tendency to digress. On McNab
he walks into an idea
for Latta. He'll shoot

all the driveways. Call it "Whole
Latta Driveways". Shoot in colour, hope.
Remain a man deeply.

+

Martin Streetpiece: Back

mid-November dogs bark
the yappiest a black hound
lives with a woman who

hearing him bark comes out
to watch me pass
the end of her yard

north to south and back
can't get through I say
gesturing *it's* blocked she says

Latta Streetpiece: Whole Latta Driveways

Traveller borrows a Nikon.

First shoot with the Nikon.

He dawdles when he gets to Latta.

Cold. Going to be short shoot.

Minus 30.

Killer on batteries.

Cold blinds.

12 driveways, one a double.

North end of Latta.

Cold catching up.

Freezing.

+

Lamont Streetpiece: Culture, Counter-culture

Nick and I smoked dope in his basement
below a print of W.C. Fields
or in the three-speed '64 Valiant
he let his friends drive playing

Judy Collins, King Crimson, The Who.
We did what
people seemed to do entered
U of R together (I dropped out)

drove to the States in his dad's car
called on his sister (who'd been
to Woodstock) and tried to find a girl
in Minot by standing next to one.

His mom was tolerant no doubt aware
of illegalities ongoing in
her rumpus room but close to Nick and good
to his friends. We knew her

smoker's cough smoker's laugh
the sort of mom we'd talk
football to in her living room
then follow Nick downstairs to smoke

our brains out on a chunk of killer hash.
A great mom I said to Nick
over coffee the other day. He said *You never
knew her when she drank*.

+

Kramer Streetpiece: Arriving

flakes destination Kramer

by bus

bye bus

by pigeons tucked into themselves

bushed

spooked by my arriving

east on Kramer

a yes/snow position

all morning no delay

snow sched

Kramer the (snow) man who owned this land

sweetheart deal with Hill the developer

who sold Twp 17 Rg 19 Sec 7 to Kramer

this was in '46 or so

knowing he'd buy it back

after it was annexed by the City

and the time to develop it

for the good of all

had arrived

gotta leave now snow

more arriving

+

Knowles Streetpiece: *American Elms Require Annual Pruning*

Man in overalls let's call him
Pete they're orange.

Pete watches off the back
of a City truck full body gear.

Say he *dangles*
he doesn't care.

Say he arcs DiPel [15]
insecticide 75 degrees. *Is it harmful?*

Pete holds a wand the only time
he holds a wand. *Not for*

humans beneficial
insects birds fish or

wildlife his business with
the undersides of trees.

I picture him
doing this.

+

Jubilee Streetpiece: Where It Goes

Turning onto Jubilee from Bell
in early June Hillsdalians commit
acts of seeing brick sunface
patch of ground cover black

and orange ball (kick-forgotten)
concrete stepping-stone *Be still
and know that I am God*
someone wrote. Further east

on Jubilee complain
is what they do about shade
this time of year. *Can't see sidewalks
for shadows* and dandelions

cause conniptions (real ones
not those phony fits my sisters
threw when they found a hole
in their nylons or ran out
of nail polish). East on Jubilee
2-hr. parking zones and dives
and wows every 50 feet. West
they sell lemonade east they back

lemons up driveways. East on Jubilee's
as much fun as a right turn
disappearing into Martin. *Gone* is where
it goes.

\+

Haultain Streetpiece: Early Music

How many times must that mother one child
lashed to her chest tip her stroller over

crusts of sidewalk circa '56. Where's
the City? Who laid stones with marigolds

inside? The mother and baby walk
to a split level for sale four hundred

thousand three bedrooms built
in 1956 on 60 feet

of frontage a bus route. A girl sits
at solo Ravel. In forty-five

minutes she and her teacher
Mrs. Schnell step outside. *Look*

that woman's going to buy that house
Mrs. Schnell says *the one beside*

the skinny kid with the three-speed.
She calls this *early music*, Mrs. Schnell —

whatever people hear people do.

+

(Gardiner S)treetpiece: Rain Dregs

Dunning Streetpiece: Doesn't Care Much About Inside

Doing Dunning done was the plan but
I met this man by accident. I said
place looks pretty green he said
been lots of rain and started

walking my way. Here was
bachelor of the prairie
days ready to talk to
whoever comes along.

He inherited the house from
his uncle Tom Carson (who bought it
from Lawrence who owned it six months)
and paid a silver dollar for

uncle Tom's Montego. *I drive the Merc maybe
twenty miles a week, twenty miles!*
Maybe you should sell it? *Well
I like to stay mobile.*

I'm doing a book on Hillsdale *Oh you are?
Too bad they built it on a bog. Can you
write us up a wind that won't blow
every shred of Dunning right here?*

*If I leave it neighbours aren't too pleased.
West wind blows it one way
sooner or later
southeast wind blows it back.*

+

Davis Streetpiece: The Name

I knew a kid Davis on Davis
a street named after his cousin
he told us. We found out the real
Davis was ambassador

to Greece. *Well no*
said Davis the kid *it was named after Bob*
Davis my cousin who built the first
two-car garage with room

to make it three. We called a
bullshit on that but Davis
stuck to his story like *long*
to *night. I'd prove it but my cousin's*

house burned down. We said *How?* He said
Somehow. All he knew was
his cousin was partner in Regina
before the first war with

a man named Hill, Walter J.[16]
father of Hill, Frederick W.
who invented *Hillsdale.*
Davis never changed

his story how could he. Fred
gave the company to his son
and Davis the street became
a cul-de-sac knobbed

on the northwest end by
fence and that house
and three-car garage like
the one in the kid's story

+

Calder Streetpiece: Sidewalks

Two sidewalks we'd each have
our own lane for bike
races past Mrs. Quirrel's

> *With respect to sidewalks,*
> *in some cities — example, Silver Heights,*
> *Winnipeg — sidewalks are not built*

house. One day
the garage door was down.
I kept on round

> *in residential areas.*
> *The greatest disadvantage*
> *is on account of small children and mothers*

the crescent a few times
who wouldn't the concrete so nice.
But I'd never seen her door

> *with children in carriages. For this reason,*
> *a sidewalk is recommended. Once*
> *the residents are used to having*

down before. Maybe her old man
didn't want me
looking in (stealing his

> *one sidewalk*
> *they find it unnecessary*
> *to have an additional one.*[17]

LawnBoss). Turns out
Mrs. Q suffocated. Don't know if she
meant to do it or not.

\+

First Anderson Streetpiece: Pins Spin
during the 2011 Scotties Tournament of Hearts

    If we lived there now
    I'd mount your pins
    by the door to the kitchen

    I recall a week at a time
    you gone some spiel
    in Humboldt or Swift Current

    home with a prize
    cocktail glasses
    blender set of sheets a recliner

    curling rock ashtray
    curling rock flask
    and stories of you and Ev

    and Edna well mom
    BC Sask
    they're playing

    the final right now
    got the tv on in your room?
    can you hear them?

Second Anderson Streetpiece: Eulogy

I salute our mom in those daytime hours
in the city after dry years and war years
and small town years. Here was
a new house, the first
she and dad ever owned, beige
split-level, nothing around but mud.

I salute our mom in those daytime hours
in her picture window, bedrooms (four)
bathrooms (two), L-shaped
living room, rumpus room and new
washer/dryer. It must have been quiet
with dad at work, us kids at school.

I salute our mom in those daytime hours.
We rushed home at noon for lunch
and dad lay down for a snooze
and we all rushed off leaving mom
the housework and shopping,
the Thursday afternoons at the rink.

I salute our mom in those daytime hours.
After school we'd practice
our piano and horn to play
"I Left My Heart in San Francisco".
Mom from the kitchen would say
"I like that one".

I salute our mom in those daytime hours
we always came home to.

+

23rd Avenue: 23 Lines, Hillsdale to Albert

Dear Albert,

They wanted me not to speak
but crows said go ahead
(wanting my apple). Their call
a laugh flew away
after a while and there I was
looking at my shadow and still
no start on this letter. When I
did get here I focussed on
the thistle and remnants of what
could have been a road. I'm not fan
of the fuckin mosquitoes, you?
Ever notice west leans
where wind blows a path
by trees west of taillights
west that steals away
your best line west
a messenger truck
hauling details west
gun it help yourself
to an edge you're done
you're driven home.

As ever, Hillsdale.

+

23rd Avenue: 23 Lines, Albert to Hillsdale

Dear Hillsdale,

23rd is "No On Street" starting June
by the former Catholic high school
friends went to the famous
Fonebone who got his face
three times in the yearbook
by shaving his head then
most of his hair then
all of it. East on 23rd behind me
signs fall down. I guess by now
you've seen *Right Here*'s a line
the school feeds the empty lot
east of the school where
the Riders once took their
outdoor pics of
hustle in the trees. I depend on
your knowing and the ruts that
lead to your streets.
I see another road leads out
and a crew. Here come
the men.

As ever, Albert.

+

**"The Road That Isn't": controversial
Twenty-fifth avenue, the no man's land
of two fighting factions of Regina's
residential subdivision, Hillsdale.**
City council put up the barricade
at the Bell Street intersection Friday.
"We had to close the avenue because
to us it no longer existed," said
City Engineer Henry Patterson.
The people on McNab were jubilant.
"That dusty avenue is a speedway
and a danger to our children who play
in backyards which back on to 25th,"
they claimed, to which the residents of Bell
spoke of the danger to their own children
from traffic now diverted through their streets.
"We bought land here because we thought it would
be quiet and safe for children," they said.
"With 25th avenue closed, now trucks
and cars are speeding up our brand new street."
Despite the barricade and ROAD CLOSED sign
a well-worn track has already been made
around the southern end of the roadblock.
This verbal warfare that has broken out
will not without a fight come to an end.

1.12 25th Avenue Streetpiece: 25 Blank Lines Found in the Leader-Post

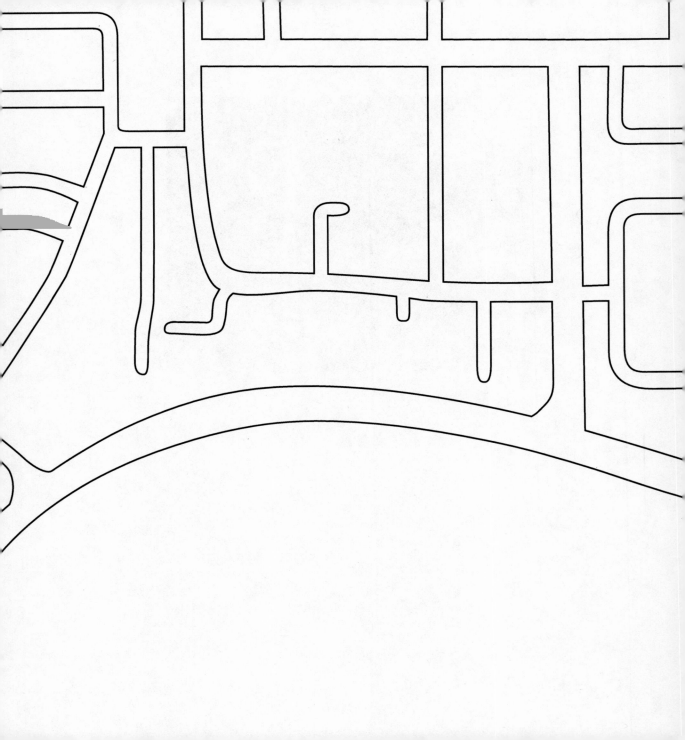

KROETSCH PARK: A SUBSUBDIVISION

a kind of madness in the recording
—**ROBERT KROETSCH,** "For Play and Entrance"

+

Paterson in Kroetsch Park

I told him I was writing a longpoem
    I may have said *long poem*
        an idea he professed to know

little about I pressed
    further on the subject of
        the docu-autogeography

around us *right now* I said
    a man in a striped vest holds up
        traffic for dumptrucks on Smith

Kroetsch shakes his whitest hair gives me
    the widest plane of his face and says
        go crazy with the trucks!

+

fragment from the *Hillsdale Bachelor's Book of Affirmation*

I too have sisters
for whom I've saved pies
they care for me

we'll take a drive
stop at cafes and
consignment stores see if

ferries still run those
stories of broken
cables are they true?

+

how I became
            a writer is break
                        my left arm Terry

tackled me wrong
            I ran home *they'll*
                        cut it off cut it off Sister #2

in training at the General
            fixed a sling out of
                        (I call it) *flannel*

in the kitchen night
            playing football
                        this all happened

right arm free to pick
            up the pencil I cried
                        at the time and now

I write this much
            and keep
                        breaking it

+

To be true
I take my Hillsdale
map to Julie's Secretarial

I find 112% to be about right Julie says
jabbing at controls *anything higher*
things can look distorted

already Calder's a pool ladder
Lake aches Gardiner
kneels for Knowles

Dunning does it McNab
nabs *see?*
says Julie

+

what is here but a kid named Wayne
                    Back and his brother Back
                                    Walley he called himself when

Mrs. Cone at Massey
                    asked his name we go
                                    play with Back Walley maybe

Wayne maybe Scott
        Staples whose dad Rod
                (we call him *Road*) answers

doors in his underwear
        just a minute he comes back
                Scott's not here

+

Rob ran deep looking back
        for the pass the elm
                bent at his crotch so hard

the lethal future imagined
        for his balls was now
                in doubt we laughed until

we all fell down Rob
        fished out his nuts from
                the bushes on Gardiner the elm

was fine in fact ever more
        potent poor Rob
                wasn't

Did you ever wear
            pointed shoes? I should have
                        kept those brogues I bought

(Florsheims) in '65.
            Indestructible! I wish
                        I was. Eva liked them

said they slowed me down.
            They weren't pointed but
                        man were they grand.

Bob I'm looking at blue sky
         and almost as high
                 the Hotel Sask in Regina.

I'm pretty sure you stayed here.
         I met a maid who said
                 she knew you a week one night

and the bartender
        with a poem you wrote
                and the waitress

wiping her hands
        and the librarian
                (she said she was)

and the masseuse
        who refused. Takes a thick hotel
                to make it in this wind.

All night the trees fell.
        You must be one of the flags Bob
          talking it up.

+

Poem for that wooden stick

            I hold in
mind this stick
                joined to my

right hand by
          my palm
imagine a survey

              stick a plan
plain
          mile south

play dirt
          play thought
right about here

            dry furrows
dry mud
           paint lids we threw

slice your hand if you
              catch one
use a stick!

            cut by the dozen from
cheap wood
          all sticks

come the way
          a line does look

houses will

    line here
        a stickdom
      stickly

+

What to Drink in Hillsdale

Big Rock Candy Martini
Gumbolaya
The Red Valiant
Manholerizer
Skydriver
'61 Special
Smells Like Jamaica Rum punch
The Shy Martini
The Sparking Lot
A Dandelionesse
(Doin' the) Hand Chive
The Honeysuckler
The Proglacial Cooler
Subourbon on the Rocks

\+

One Afternoon at the Regina Cemetery

Lizzie Anne Nelson
   Lucretia Ann Beazely
      Matilda Falconer

Julius Dorn (more Falconers) Dalton
   John Anderson who died
      on my birthday in '08 only

seventeen how does he
   get here and two
      lovers in t-shirts

blonde hair if here
   flowers move
      it's the horny dead

oh *look* Mrs. Gleedahl
        says through her picture
               window one finger hooked at

the curtains *a magazine rack*
        that boy made at school!
              somebody tell her it took 2nd

prize at Regina fair to a
                    pie-lifter size of a shovel
                                        and sits for fifty years beside

the boy's favourite chair
                    on which (you knew
                                        this was coming) he rocked

the Gleedahl girl Lenore
                    who never said
                                        no more

+

Acrostic for Bob (stick)

rare is thè aftern
oon
bob n
ext door *w*
ri
ting poems I love it! who
knows when I'll
read him "elegy f
or Wong Toy" again h
e was weak and sa
t out
side I pla
ce
him here with the raven

that flood of '74 the Cranes
             in borrowed canoe launched
                          from Langley and Jubilee

water takes them over
             sunken streets neighbours
                          stranded on roofs a man

in a tub two small girls
             in a fibreglass pool a guy straddling
                          twelve feet of pine the Stevensons

steering their upside-down *coupé* (Amanda S.
             her knitting along she never
                          got to how could she) Mrs. Crane

call her Jean had wondered
             how she would go
                          this was it? the lake

lasted four days and nights
             and set her down
                          by her back door her husband

call him Tony not far
             away their minds
                          full of water

\+

Play at the Plate

pounding home plate Lloyd
           acts the Babe *how many*
                      days and nights do you

want me here? he slams
           first pitch to deep right a sure
                      round-tripper by the time

he reaches second the ball's
           fired back in "big Lloyd" (he calls
                      himself) rounds third the catcher

waits ➜ ball ➜ catch ➜ Lloyd
           knocks off her glove and mask
                      touches home *you ok Eva?*

someone hollers *yeah fine* she turns
           to Lloyd *as for you*
                      asshole you're out

\+

Tree-piece Suite

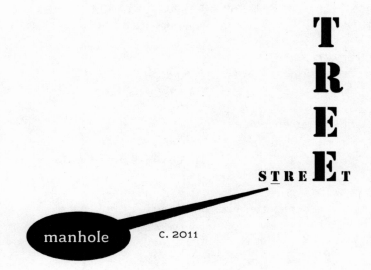

T
R
E
S T R E E T

c. 1961

T
R
E
E
S T R E E t

c. 1986

T
R
E
E
S T R E E t

manhole   c. 2011

+

one way to say it is
        she and I meet in low light
                at the King's Hotel a band

no décor just a band low light next
        we're kissing the sun's ass
                in front of her mom's place on Pasqua

still we'd be kissing if
        I had enough gas one night
                we take a bedroom in

that townhouse on 18th
        real bodies I cry out
                or just cry a few months later

we get a place on Smith Street
        she kicks me out I don't know why
                she buggers off or I do

to Calgary 40 years
        after that I'm sitting down
                for a crap I open

this handwritten envelope
        from Calgary *Dear Gerry*
                I hope you're sitting down

when you read this
        the letter goes on to say
                you were kind I do recall

kindness not that
                    I knew why *I wouldn't mind*
                                        a chat says her letter here memories

slip free swirl erratic
                    and nasty *come on we're not*
                                        so bad but see their pointed sticks

hooks and looks their handbooks
                    on how to cause fresh pain
                                        later that same letter

Here's my number. Do call. For sure
                    and here's the lowest drawer of the deepest desk
                                        here's that file that says

DO NOT DO NOT
                    EVER DO NOT
                                        EVER AGAIN READ.

+

Dying on the longest day
writing on the longest day on Darke.

It's ago.
You don't want

ceremony of any kind
but to hell with that.

Everybody's Business in Kroetsch Park

    Shipanski Flood 'n Fire
    Beetle and Sons Irritation
    Clair's Fashion: We'll Layer You!

    Bob's Moving
    Ophelia's Dirt 'n Stone
    Stick & Sons: You Can Pick Us Up!

    Paterson's Myth and Mapping
    Rusty's Plumbing — We'll Get to You In Time!
    Grandpa & Sons Tombstones: We'll Bury You Right Here!

Have you noticed wildlife Kroetsching on your urban space? Call us! [18]

YOU ARE NOWTHEN
LEAVING HILLSDALE

You wear Portuguese wool and Italian wool.
You drink downtown Regina tea.
You imagine Hillsdale under
four or five feet of snow.
Everyone has garages now.
Last month SaskPower cleaned out
the easements when a couple
of houses exploded.
The Baptist church took out
four lindens on Munroe
and traffic to the rink has eased.

You see yourself as a
man in a
boy in an
end to a book.

You're after.

Notes

1   Says Fred Hill, President of McCallum-Hill, the developer.

2   Says my friend Carl, a farmer.

3   After Daphne Marlatt, *Steveston*.

4   Says Dad, directing relatives to our place from Albert street.

5   We were protestant and blonde.

6   What, I wonder, did he want to walk in the front door and see?

7   Says Bobby Cheswick's dad.

8   Flo told me.

9   A variation of a story told to me by David Carpenter.

10   After a poem by Aziz Hagini (items from July 13/09 notebook).

11   Don Kerr, *My Own Places: Poems on John Constable*.

12   for Brenda Schmidt "in honour of that duck in your book."

13   One kid puts it, years later. He'd gone to McVeety in north Hillsdale and met the real Marion McVeety, long-time Regina Public teacher known for her firm hand — not allowing a single snicker, for example, when Billy Rivers peed his pants in her Grade Two classroom at Lakeview school.

14   José Saramago, *Journey to Portugal*.

15   DiPel 2X DF.

16   No relation to the author.

17   "Report on Hillsdale Subdivision Located in the City of Regina", Haddin, Davis & Brown Ltd., April, 1955.

18   After CBC Radio host Laurie Brown, "The Signal", 11:16 pm, Monday, July 12, 2010.

Acknowledgements

I'm grateful to Hillsdalians past and present, including Rick Ast, Jack Boan, Cam Bower, Jean Cogger, Donald Kramer, Thomas Gentles, Karla Gritzfeld, Martin Grudnitski, Fred and Bev Hill, Vicky Kangles, Pat Krause, Katherine Lawrence, George Mollard, Herb Padwick, Phyllis Schwann, Gord Staseson, Mary Vetter, Peggy Wakeling, Dick and Sandy Wiest, Eva Williams, Bryan Wyrostok, the anonymous couple on Martin, and the non-Hillsdalians (but they've been there) Gordon Gardiner, Randy Johner, Bob Linner, D'arcy Schenk, Joni Thue, Michael Trussler, and Dianne Warren.

A tip of the cap to my three sisters, June Danngren, Fay Karp, and Susan Van Gasbeck, who are little like the sisters in this book (except for the good parts).

This book took shape in Hillsdale and in residencies at Convento de São Francisco, Mértola, Portugal; Saskatchewan Writers/Artists Retreats at Emma Lake and St. Peter's Abbey; The Leighton Colony at The Banff Centre; Hawthornden International Retreat for Writers, Lasswade, Scotland (thanks to a Travel Grant from the Canada Council for the Arts); at Sage Hill Writing Experience; and during travels in Portugal, Spain, Great Britain, western Canada and Hillsdale itself. Thanks to all companions.

My employer, Luther College at the University of Regina, provided invaluable support.

Working with Daphne Marlatt at Sage Hill Writing Experience taught me plenty about this book.

Thanks to Al Van Gasbeck for the loan of the Nikon. All photographs in this book are by G.Hill, except one by Tom Gentles and three found in the Saskatchewan Provincial Archive, used with permission.

I salute these books so useful at different times and in different ways: *feria: a poempark*, Oana Avasilichioaei; *Kerrisdale Elegies*, George Bowering; *Building Suburbia: Green Fields and Urban Growth, 1820–2000*, Dolores Hayden; *The Death and Life of Great American Cities*, Jane Jacobs; *My Own Places: Poems on John Constable*, Don Kerr; *The Ledger*, Robert Kroetsch; *Steveston* and *The Given*, Daphne Marlatt; *An Innocent in Ireland: Curious Rambles and Singular Encounters*, David McFadden; *The City in History: Its Origins, Its Transformations, and Its Prospects*, Lewis Mumford; *The Martyrology, Book 5*, bp Nichol; *The Maximus Poems*, Charles Olson; *The Collected Works of Billy the Kid*, Michael Ondaatje; *Dart*, Alice Oswald; *Life in the Canopy*, Bruce Rice; *Jeremiah, Ohio*, Adam Sol; *Journey to Portugal*, José Saramago (thanks to Annette Bower for the loan); *Deepwater Vee*, Melanie Siebert; *Wood Mountain* Poems, Andy Suknaski; *Falling Into Place*, John Terpstra; *Paterson*, W.C. Williams; *Places Far From Ellesmere*, Aritha van Herk; and *The Organization Man*, William H. Whyte.

Although Hillsdale has existed for almost 60 years, and the author lived there for half of them, Hillsdale as it appears in this book is a place of imagination. Readers are advised to take caution, if they don't mind, with assumptions about the truth of names, events or locations they meet here. This is a work of fact made of fiction and fiction made of fact. Some names and situations have been changed, some made up, some forgotten.

Selections from "Streetpieces" appeared as part of Series Nine of the Alfred Gustav Press chapbook series, edited by David Zieroth.

Other Hillsdale text and images appeared as "Hillsdale, a Map", by Gerald Hill and Jared Carlson, published by Silver Birch Design in 2012. Thanks to Jared for the ongoing inspiration of his work, still evident.

Finally, a tip of the cap to Don Kerr, Poet Laureate of Saskatchewan, for his sharp and friendly walk through this material, and to the staff and Board of NeWest Press for their enthusiasm and care.

Gerald Hill is a two-time winner of the
Saskatchewan Book Award for Poetry.
His previous collection with NeWest Press
was *14 Tractors*. Active as both organizer of
and participant in workshops, conferences
and courses, Gerald teaches English and
Creative Writing at Luther College at the
University of Regina, amid spells of readings
and writing residencies in Canada and Europe.